Tri in PARADISE

by Jerlyn Thomas

Text copyright © 2020 by Design Lady LLC (designlady.com)
Cover art and interior illustrations copyright © 2020 by Jerlyn Thomas
(Reprinted 2021)

Visit http://commuteartist.com for more information.

This book is dedicated to all the kids who dare to "tri."

Thanks to my husband Michael, who loves the triathlon as much as I do. We hope to inspire our daughter Mattis to love it too.

Days before her big races, she visits her favorite physical therapy office to get "fresh legs."

Everytime I call it a big race Mom smiles and says it's small by comparison.

"It's called a sprint."

	Swim	Bike	Run
Supersprint	400 m	10 km	2.5 km
Sprint	(750 m)	(20 km)	(5 km)
Olympic	1500 m	40 km	10 km
Mid	2.5 km	80 km	20 km
Lon	4 km	120 km	30 km
Iron	3.8 km	180 km	42 km

Her bike gets its own suitcase.

After we drop them off at the airport, we won't see our bags again until we get to St. Croix.

Mom and Dad pack a carry on for me with my own bottle, so I won't get thirsty during our flight.

Mom puts her bike together when we get to St. Croix—to make sure she hasn't forgotten anything. She says that would be the worst.

She packed a flat kit, just in case she has to change her tires during the race.

Then, we go to pick up her race bibs.

She lays out her kit and snacks to take with her in the morning. I help her cross off the items on the list.

When we get there, we can see all the bikes lined up from outside the gate. I can see Mom's bike in the middle with her kit.

Mom has to swim to where the race starts so she considers that her warm up.

I sit on the dock with Dad. There are many colorful fish and I can see my feet in the clear water.

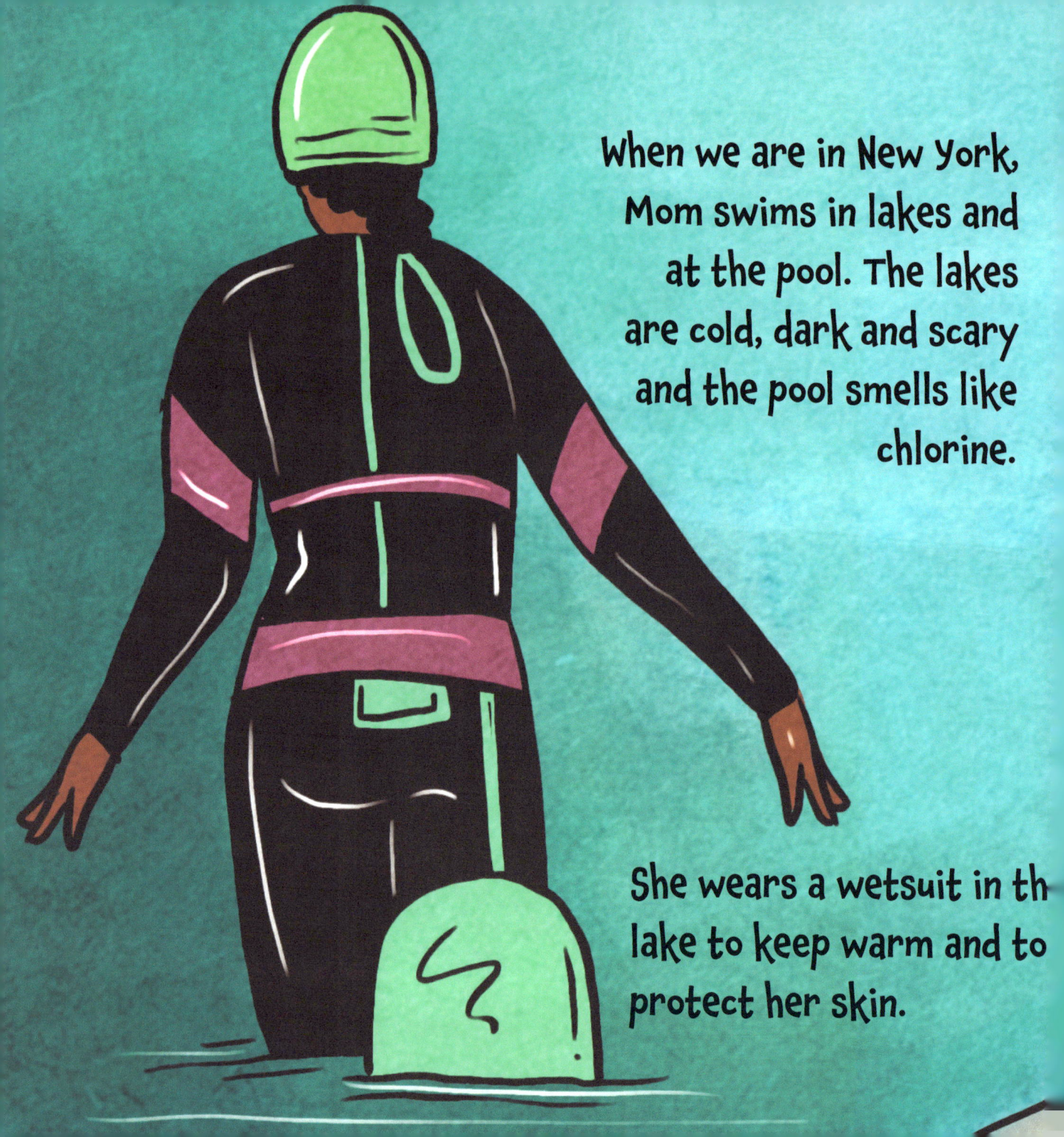

When we are in New York, Mom swims in lakes and at the pool. The lakes are cold, dark and scary and the pool smells like chlorine.

She wears a wetsuit in th lake to keep warm and to protect her skin.

When I swim with her,
I wear colorful floaties.

Back on St. Croix, the announcer calls Mom's group for the race.

She jumps into the ocean and starts to swim.

Dad and I wave at her as she passes us. Grandma and some of her friends join us and bring some signs.

When we are at home in New York, she runs further than that sometimes.

We got back just in time to see Mom finish as her name is announced.

She records her time and is excited that she won her age group. My favorite part is when she lets me wear her medal.

One day, I would love to race like Mommy does, but she promised that after the race we are going to get some treats, my second favorite part!

About the author and illustrator

I started running in 2008 and traveled across the United States to participate in numerous distance races. In 2015, I tried a triathlon and got hooked right away.

I fell in love with the training. I found a coach to teach me swimming techniques and I invested in a beautiful road bike. I also kept running and have run two 50-mile races since then.

Eventually, I began observing the lack of diversity, as I started placing at specific distances. I took it upon myself to attempt to enter more races.

At races I try to wear vibrant colors to stand out and wave at kids that I see in the crowds. I wrote

this book to inspire my daughter to try triathlons as she grows up, I also want to encourage young girls who don't usually see athletes like me in books.

After I started racing, I came across amazing triathletes like Sika Henry and Max Fennell and ultramarathon runner Mirna Valerio who are redefining the world of distance sports and what athletes usually look like.

I hope reading this book will help motivate companies to sponsor programs to help underprivileged kids get access to pools, equipment and racing. My goal is to inspire others (including my daughter Mattis) to come to love the sport as much as I do.